Contents

D0001513

NOTE: The images in this book are meant to convey visually the spirit of Africa's wildlife, and are therefore not captioned. For full descriptions of the photos *see page 44.*

African Wildlife

WARREN J. HALLIBURTON

EDITED BY
SUSAN M. GROSSMAN

CRESTWOOD HOUSE
NEW YORK

MAXWELL MACMILLAN CANADA
TORONTO

MAXWELL MACMILLAN INTERNATIONAL
NEW YORK OXFORD SINGAPORE SYDNEY

ACKNOWLEDGMENTS

All photos courtesy of Magnum Photos.

Special thanks to Laura Straus for her assistance in putting this project together.

PHOTO CREDITS: COVER: *Burt Glinn*; *Burt Glinn* 13, 17, 21, 30, 34, 36, 38; *Ian Berry* 5, 6, 29; *Jean Gaumy* 9; *Ingeborg Lippman* 14, 35, 41; *Simon Cherpitel* 15, 18; *Michael K. Nichols* 23, 24, 27, 31, 45; *Rene Burri* 25; *Dennis Stock* 26; *Bruno Barbey* 33; *Alex Webb* 42

Cover design, text design and production: William E. Frost Associates Ltd.

Library of Congress Cataloging-in-Publication Data

Halliburton, Warren J.
     African wildlife / by Warren J. Halliburton;
edited by Susan M. Grossman. — 1st ed.
p. cm. — (Africa today)
     Summary: Describes the four major habitats found on the African continent and the animals that live there.
     ISBN 0-89686-674-2
     1. Habitat (Ecology) — Africa — Juvenile literature. 2. Wildlife conservation — Africa — Juvenile literature. 3. Habitat conservation — Africa — Juvenile literature. [1. Zoology—Africa. 2. Habitat (Ecology) — Africa.] I. Grossman, Susan M. II. Title. III. Series: Africa today
QH541.264.A35H35 1992
591.5'264'096—dc20   91-43514

CRESTWOOD HOUSE   MAXWELL MACMILLAN CANADA, INC.
MACMILLAN PUBLISHING COMPANY   1200 Eglinton Avenue East
866 Third Avenue   Suite 200
New York, NY 10022   Don Mills, Ontario M3C 3N1

Macmillan Publishing Company is part of the Maxwell Communication Group of Companies.
First edition
Printed in the United States of America

1   2   3   4   5   6   7   8   9   10

Introduction

A Fragile Ecology

Threatened Animals, Threatened Land

Africa is a complicated place. This huge continent, nearly the size of North America and Europe combined, is a land of contrasts: Sand, snow and jungle exist alongside rich farmland and grassy plains. Africans in cities park luxurious cars outside elegant restaurants while Tuaregs in flowing robes shepherd goats across the largest desert in the world. Nature follows its timeless rhythms within sight of the gleaming towers of cities, and lions in national parks nap on the roofs of tourists' cars.

Africa is in many ways a land of plenty, teeming with more wildlife than anywhere else in the world. But Africa is also a land in danger, threatened by famine and the destruction of its environment. Animals are often in direct competition with people for food and space. In this contest, wildlife usually loses. The result is that there are 900 species now facing extinction in Africa.

The biggest problem is loss of **habitat**, the place where a particular animal can live. Habitats are often lost because humans, needing new places to live and grow food or graze cattle and goats, expand into the area. Domestic animals are a real problem in Africa's fragile ecology. Cattle, important in many tribal economies as symbols of wealth and status and in national economies as meat animals, will graze an area bare. In places where vegetation is already sparse, they leave behind patches of desert where nothing can live.

Humans log the forests for hardwood, cut trees for firewood, and set fires to make clearings in a process known as **slash and burn**. Slash-and-burn fires run wild, killing vast areas of vegetation. When the trees are gone, the topsoil runs off, leaving areas that can no longer support growth. The soil is carried into waterways, where it kills aquatic life. In dry areas where there were few trees to begin with, the destruction of the trees creates desert. This process, called **desertification**, is a great problem in Africa today.

Humans slaughter animals directly too. Hoofed animals have been blamed for carrying disease to domestic livestock and humans, and until the 1950s, when pesticides brought insect problems under control, there were wholesale killings of the great herds. And it is still legal to kill even protected animals when they threaten farms.

Poaching is a huge problem in Africa. This takes place on a large organized level, as in the illegal ivory trade, and on a small individual level that nonetheless adds up to countless animals killed. Tribespeople who have always lived off animal products consider it their right to hunt the animals, and it is hard to convince them that they cannot, that there are limited numbers of animals left.

In a place where famine stalks the land, it is hard to interest people in the hardships faced by wildlife whose territory is disappearing. It is one thing for the world to say, "Yes, we should stop killing the elephants." It is another thing for a farmer who has just watched a herd of elephants grind his crops into the dust.

Conservation

Even so, Africa has set aside huge areas of land for the protection of wildlife. In Africa, there are many legal categories for these areas, the most important national designation being "national park." There are also forest and game preserves. In countries where it is legal to "own" the animals that are on a person's land, such as South Africa, there are private preserves as well.

Despite the conflict between people and animals, Africa has a long history of conservation. The first organization was set up in 1883, the year the last quagga, an African wild ass, died. Today, many Africans are recognizing that the animals won't last forever unless they and the land are cared for.

Different countries are working on different solutions. In South Africa, individuals harvest the meat of just enough animals on their land to keep numbers steady, and they sell live animals to restock land. Making preservation a matter of profit has led to spectacular conservation successes in this country.

In many preserves across the continent, rare or threatened animals are increasing their numbers. In Kenya, rangers are thinking of new ways to conserve. For instance, they are moving black rhinos from large areas to small areas that can more easily be defended from poachers. But some areas must keep their space if they are to exist as ecological systems. Serengeti National Park in Tanzania is one of these and has been declared a world heritage site.

The Habitats

Africa has examples of almost any type of habitat you can name: deserts, coastal areas, lowlands, grasslands, woodlands, forests, swamps, tropical rain forests, and even bamboo forests and alpine areas.

There is a very general progression from dry to lush areas as you move toward the center of the country from the north and south. In the extreme north and south, there are fringes of a Mediterranean-type environment. Further in, there is the great Sahara Desert in the north and the Kalahari in the south. These areas are bordered by semidesert steppe areas — the northern one is known as the Sahel, and the southern as the veldt. These blend into the savannas, the grasslands of Africa, and the savannas themselves progress from short grass dotted with thorny acacia trees to tall grass and eventually to woodland and forest. In the west is a belt of rain forest; to the east, mountain vegetation.

The animals of Africa can be roughly grouped in terms of the habitat they spend the most time in. These habitats are the **savanna**, the **forest**, the **wetlands** and the **desert**. It should be remembered, though, that few countries have a uniform kind of environment, and most animals range through more than one habitat.

The Savanna

The Land

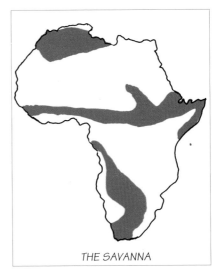

THE SAVANNA

The savannas—the grasslands of Africa—are the richest in wildlife of any grasslands on earth. Herds of antelope of many kinds crop the grass alongside zebras and giraffes. Wildebeest migrate across the plains in herds sometimes numbering in the thousands. Cape buffalo graze by water holes, and prehistoric-looking black rhinos nibble leaves from bushes while white rhinos graze. Elephants stride through the acacia thickets and oat grass, afraid of nothing but humans. The herbivores, or plant eaters, are preyed on by lions, leopards, cheetahs, hyenas and wild dogs. Jackals and vultures scavenge the remains. Small mammals scurry through the grass along with countless insects, snakes and lizards. The sky is filled with hunting birds.

The savanna, which makes up two-fifths of Africa, curves from the Atlantic coast just south of the Sahara across eastern Africa and westward to the coast south of the Congo basin. The grasslands flourish in the countries of Botswana, Kenya, Namibia, Rwanda, South Africa, Tanzania, Zaire, Zambia and Zimbabwe. Not all grassland is the same — there are different types of savanna, progressing from semidesert all the way through woodland.

The driest type of savanna is semidesert. The largest stretch of this, the Sahel, lies just south of the Sahara and merges with the desert. In this region, grasses disappear during the long dry season but reappear with the rains. Another type of dry savanna, such as that making up southern Africa's Kalahari, generally borders the semidesert areas and is a mixture of tall and short grasses dotted with tough, thorny trees and shrubs. The trees of the savanna are primarily different types of acacia, thorny and feathery-leaved. An occasional baobab rises from the plain. Huge and ancient — they may live for up to 2,500 years — baobabs house many **nocturnal** animals and are thought by some tribes to be houses of the spirits. Many acacia trees have been decimated by elephants, especially in Kenya's Tsavo National Park.

Where there is more moisture, the grass grows taller, over three feet in height, and more abundantly. These grassy savannas stretch east to the Nile, across the continent between the Sahel and the equator, and are also found in Zaire, eastern Africa and parts of the south. On the margins of the forests, the trees increase to the point where the savanna becomes woodland. This type of habitat stretches from Cameroon in West Africa to northeastern Zaire, and from western Angola to the Indian Ocean.

The Plant Eaters

The Great Herds: The Zebra, the Giraffe and the Antelope
Africa is known for its great herds of plant-eating hoofed animals, the zebras, antelopes and giraffes, which in turn feed the meat eaters.

Zebras are really striped wild horses. The common, or Burchell's, zebra is found anyplace within a day's reach of water in eastern and southern Africa. These animals are grazers that sometimes congregate in huge herds made up of family units consisting of a male, or stallion,

and a small group of females, or mares, sharing their grazing areas with giraffe and antelope, especially wildebeest. In the dry season they migrate with the wildebeest, searching for food and water.

There are several different kinds of giraffe, each having a different pattern of spots. Giraffes eat the leaves from the high branches of trees.

There are more kinds of antelope in Africa than anywhere else in the world. The most numerous antelope of the plains are Thompson's gazelle and the larger Grant's gazelle. These graceful animals depend on their speed and agility for protection and are the main food of many **predators**. Other antelopes range in size from the huge eland, weighing almost a ton, to the tiny royal antelope, less than a foot high. Antelopes' habits and environments vary as widely.

The wildebeest, or gnu, is a strange-looking antelope known for gathering in huge herds of up to several thousand animals for seasonal migrations. However, the great migrations of Africa, although they still take place on the Serengeti, are almost a thing of the past, as fences crisscross the continent and prevent animals from following the ancient routes to water, and as humans affect the herds' environment.

The Rhino The rhino is one of Africa's most impressive herbivores. There are two kinds of rhinos in Africa, the white rhino and the black rhino (both are actually gray). The white, a grass eater, stands five to six feet at the shoulder and weighs more than two tons. The black rhino is

smaller, more agile, and is mostly a browser of leaves. The black rhino can be found in all kinds of environments, from dry bush country to mountain forests.

Unfortunately the rhinoceros's existence in the wild is threatened. White rhinos have been exterminated in East Africa. The black rhino's range has been steadily decreasing, mostly because of competition with humans for living space, and because the areas they live in are often prime grazing areas for cattle. More recently the main reason for their endangerment has become poaching — rhino horn is considered valuable in Asia, and one horn is equivalent to three years' salary for a typical African villager. Black rhinos are now found only in a few tiny sanctuaries.

The Meat Eaters

The Lion When many people think of African animals, it is the majestic lion that they see. These tremendously powerful carnivores can bring down animals weighing three-quarters of a ton. Although only half the weight of the males, lionesses make most of the kills.

Since zebra and most antelope run faster than the lion's top speed of around 35 miles per hour, the cats prefer to hunt stealthily or cooperatively. Despite their power, they are relatively inefficient hunters, sometimes injured by the flying hooves and sharp horns of their prey, and they often scavenge. Lions are the only social cats and live in prides made up of 3 to 30 related females dominated by one male, although there may be a young male or two.

As with many animals, lions, although protected, are no longer plentiful outside the wild animal parks of Africa. Lions are prone to starvation, and less than half the cubs born survive their first year. But

humans, directly or indirectly, are the lion's worst enemy. And as the great grazing herds decrease in number, so do the animals that prey on them.

The Dogs: The African Wild Dog and the Jackal The hunting dogs of the African plains include African wild dogs, jackals and foxes. African wild dogs, which are superb, cooperative hunters, look and act very little like domestic, or pet, dogs. Although protected, they haven't bounced back from years of attempted extermination, and the future of these fascinating animals is uncertain. Jackals behave very much like domestic dogs. They will eat almost anything, even vegetables, and wait for leftovers around the kill of a larger predator as well as scavenging around human homesteads.

The Hyena Hyenas look something like dogs, but they are actually related to the mongoose. There are three kinds of hyena: spotted, striped and brown. The spotted hyena, the one most people are familiar with, is found in all types of habitats. Its strange cry has led it to be called the laughing hyena. Because hyenas are "the undertakers of the plains," disposing of the remains of dead animals, they are often associated with death. But the hyena's bad reputation is undeserved. It is the smaller striped hyena of North Africa that is primarily a **scavenger**, and it performs a valuable function in cleaning areas of **carrion**, or dead flesh. Spotted hyenas, by contrast, are efficient group hunters with a complex social system.

Birds, Insects and Reptiles

It is easy for the large mammals to overshadow the smaller animals of the savanna, but this habitat teems with birds, insects and other forms of life. The many kinds of birds feed on seeds, insects, other birds and small mammals. There are more kinds of hunting birds in Africa than anywhere else: The sky is often filled with eagles, hawks, buzzards and vultures. Ground-dwelling birds are common — ostriches, tall secretary birds, guinea fowls and bustards strut among the scattered trees and bushes.

The life of the savanna dwellers and the land itself is tied together, smallest to largest. The smallest savanna dwellers, the insects, are vitally important in maintaining the savanna. Ants, beetles and termites are the main food source for many animals, and the huge mounds that termites live in landscape the plains. With plenty of insects and small animals to eat and underground shelters to live in, the savanna is also rich in reptile life.

Parks

Protected savanna areas can be found in Botswana, Kenya, Namibia, Rwanda, South Africa, Tanzania, Zaire, Zambia and Zimbabwe. Eastern Africa is especially rich in wildlife, and tourism in these countries is big business — Kenya alone has protected wildlife parks equal in area to

Switzerland. Some of its best-known areas are Amboseli National Park, which is known for its elephants, as is Tsavo. The Masai Mara Game Reserve is the dry-weather grazing ground for the great herds of wildebeest that will migrate to Tanzania's Serengeti National Park to eat the grass following the seasonal rain. The vast Serengeti ecosystem includes these two parks, and the animals of these short-grass plains are probably what most people think of when they envision African wildlife.

To the south, Botswana devotes 17 percent of its area to wildlife protection, one of the highest percentages of any country. Namibia's Etosha National Park is best known for its elephant population and is the site of seasonal migrations by wildebeest and other antelope and zebra. South Africa's Kruger is the area's largest national park, almost the size of Massachusetts. These parks represent only a few of Africa's protected savanna habitats.

2

The Forest

The Land

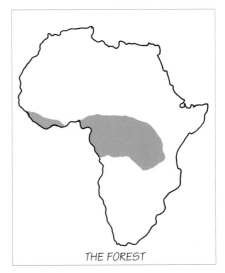

THE FOREST

A black-and-white colobus monkey launches itself from a branch to land in a tree 30 feet below. A leopard glares up at it from a limb, snarling, before returning to feed on the duiker antelope it has wedged in the fork of the tree. Far above, where there is sunlight, butterflies float among bright flowers, and parrots flash through the leaves. Far below a huge bongo antelope pauses, its feet silent in the soft carpet of rotting vegetation making up the forest's floor. Sixty feet above, monkeys and squirrels chatter among the highway of branches and leaves that make up the middle canopy of the forest.

This is the tropical rain forest. Covering seven percent of the continent, it is a belt stretching from Uganda's western boundary across the Congo River basin to the Atlantic Ocean in the west and north to Gabon, Cameroon and the southeastern coast of Nigeria. Other types of forest make up another two percent of the continent — swamp forests, which grow along riverbanks and get their moisture from the river rather than from rain; and montane forests, which grow in cooler, drier areas and cover all the major mountains of Africa.

At first glance, it seems as though there are not many animals in the dense forest. This is because many of them don't live at ground level, and those that do are camouflaged among the tangled bushes and tree roots. The animals of the forest are beautifully adapted to their environment. Some of them have special features that fit them for **arboreal** — tree-dwelling — life. Many forest dwellers can also be found in other habitats.

This special environment is disappearing from the world at a rate of two to six percent per year. This means that the forest could be gone within 50 years. When trees are cut down or burned, an irreplaceable habitat, and the animals that live there, are lost forever.

The Plant Eaters

The Elephant Elephants are the largest land animals in the world, standing more than 11 feet tall and weighing upward of six tons. They can be found in a wide range of habitats south of the Sahara: In semidesert, forest, open woodland, and grassy plain. In some ways, elephants are very much like humans: They are highly intelligent and have a complex social organization. They live nearly as long as humans and enjoy a long childhood. They also "talk" to each other and, like humans, they change their environment, smashing clearings in forests and converting woodlands to grasslands with their feeding. They eat every food crop people can grow and every plant that livestock can eat.

These habits have put the elephant into direct competition with humans for food and space, and the result is that elephants in the wild are threatened with extinction within this century. Elephants are also illegally killed for their ivory tusks, which are sold for huge profits.

Elephants are protected in many national parks. However, because they are destructive feeders that kill the trees they eat, they have devastated many of the areas that were designed to protect them, such as Kenya's Tsavo. Also, elephants need a great deal of room in which to find food, and pressure from growing human populations has been reducing the size of national parks. In some places, elephants have been destroyed to preserve the land and to keep other animals from starving to death, a controversial measure taken in Tsavo and in Uganda's Murchison Falls National Park in the mid-1960s. Although many people are working on preserving both the land and the elephants, the problem is far from solved.

The Primates

The forests abound with primates. Of these, gorillas and chimpanzees are exclusively forest-dwellers, while baboons and monkeys can be found in a wide range of habitats.

The Gorilla Gorillas and chimpanzees are apes. They inhabit mostly western rain forests. The mountain gorilla holds out in Rwanda, the southwestern tip of Uganda, and the Virunga volcanoes of Zaire. These apes become more and more rare as humans expand into their habitat. The mountain gorilla is especially threatened. In the 1970s there were only 250 left, but it looks as though their numbers are beginning to increase. The largest living primate, the gorilla is nevertheless a gentle, intelligent vegetarian that lives in family groups and spends its day wandering in search of food, resting and interacting with other members of the group. The gorilla's only enemies are leopards and humans.

The Chimpanzee Chimpanzees can be found in some Ugandan lowland forests and in a few small groups on the shores of Lake Tanganyika. The most intelligent apes, they communicate with a large variety of sounds, make tools, and have humanlike facial expressions. Although shorter than humans, they are much stronger, and they can pick up objects with

their feet as well as their hands. Chimps travel in groups of about 20, and babies stay with their mothers for four years. They eat mostly fruit and nuts, but occasionally eat insects and small mammals. These animals are in need of protection in the wild as their habitats disappear.

The Baboon   The baboon has a wide range of environments, from semidesert to woodland. Weighing between 30 and 90 pounds, baboons are intelligent monkeys that live in troops of up to 300 led by a few males. Baboons are serious competitors with humans for food because they destroy crops. They also eat meat, killing other monkeys, birds and young antelope, and it appears that they sometimes kill for sport. Yet they are also playful—for instance, jumping onto an antelope's back for a ride.

The Monkeys   Several kinds of monkeys live in the forest. The largest family of monkeys is the guenon. Small to medium-sized, they are mostly arboreal. Larger and more impressive in appearance are the two kinds of black-and-white colobus monkeys, which have beautiful white "capes" of fur. Along with the smaller red colobus, these monkeys are unique in being entirely herbivorous. Most monkeys are **omnivores**, eating birds' eggs, flowers, frogs, fruits, grasses, insects, lizards, nuts and roots.

The Meat-Eaters

The Leopard The only large forest predator, up to eight feet from nose to tail, the leopard is silent, elusive and mostly nocturnal. Leopards can also be found in many other environments, ranging all the way from semidesert to high mountains. They do not, however, live on the open plains where there are no trees, because lions will kill them if they catch them on the ground and because they store their food in trees. These strong, fierce cats are willing to scavenge and will eat almost any kind of meat. Because of their adaptability, leopards can be found very close to cities. Leopards can pursue monkeys through the trees, and in places where leopards have been killed off, monkeys have caused great crop damage. Many consider leopards to be the carnivore most dangerous to humans.

Birds and Insects

Most forest birds are brightly colored, but because they don't live at ground level, they are more often heard than seen. Touracos are large, often bright green with brilliant red flight feathers. They hop along branches, working higher and higher until they glide to another tree. Black-and-white hornbills are also large, and their heavy wing beats can often be heard even if the birds aren't visible. Brightly colored parrots flash through the trees, screaming harshly. These intelligent, powerful birds are in danger of extinction because they are captured to be exported as pets and because they damage crops and are therefore killed. The smaller parakeets make their home in the forest as well.

Also brightly colored are the insects of the rain forest. The different types of insects living here is staggering, numbering in tens of millions, and it's assumed that there are many that have never yet been seen. In the forest, where there are no large scavengers, insects do the vital job of disposing of carrion. Other kinds of insects break down the dead plant material that makes up the forest floor.

Parks

Some of the forest-area parks in Africa are Kenya's Abedare, Mount Elgon and Mount Kenya; Rwanda's Volcano National Park; Tanzania's Arusha, Gombe Stream and Mount Kilimanjaro; and Zaire's Virunga. Abedare contains the famous Treetops hotel, a structure built around a salt lick that attracts many animals, some of them rare and otherwise almost never seen. Mount Elgon is a huge, extinct volcano, and many of its plants are giant versions of those usually found in alpine environments. Mount Kenya is the second-highest mountain in Africa, and its wildlife is scattered and rarely seen. Volcano National Park is the home of the mountain gorilla, and in fact the park was expanded specifically to include the gorilla's range and thus protect it. This range extends into Zaire's Parc des Virungas. Uganda's Impenetrable Forest is the other home of the mountain gorilla. Gombe Stream National Park is another park important in one animal's protection — it is the home of the chimpanzees that naturalist Jane Goodall has studied, acquainting the world with the qualities of humankind's closest relative.

3

The Wetlands

The Land

Many of Africa's wetlands are part of a larger habitat — a swamp within a forest, a narrow swamp forest fringing the shores of a savanna river, an oasis in a desert. And Africa has many lake regions, some of them saltwater, draining off the Nile. The wetlands are visited by large herbivores that come to drink and the carnivores that come to hunt them. But the permanent residents of the wetlands are the animals that must live in and near water, such as hippos, crocodiles

THE WETLANDS

and otters. Some antelope, as well, live only in wet areas — such as the large sitatunga, whose hooves are splayed so that the antelope can use them like snowshoes to cross the marshy ground. Other animals, like the buffalo, may live on the savanna or in the forest, but must have water nearby. The wetlands are also a paradise for birds, and here are found spectacular flocks of flamingos and a host of other fowl.

The Plant Eaters

The Hippo The hippo is a huge relative of the pig. The third-largest land animal, it weighs as much as 7,000 pounds. These animals, which spend most of their time wallowing in marshlands, ponds, rivers and lakes, use their horny lips as mowers to shave the grass and water plants they eat. Hippos are important in maintaining the wetlands ecology because the vegetable matter in their waste products supports the microscopic aquatic plants and animals called plankton and the chain of animals that feed on them. Hippos are considered even more dangerous than the notoriously fierce buffalo, since they are huge, short-tempered, nimble in water — and armed with razor-sharp teeth. River hippos live in herds of from five to 30 animals. Except in cool, wet weather, they spend their days partly submerged, often with birds and turtles perched on their backs. At night, they may roam in search of food. During the mating season, male hippos have fierce fights, with their powerful teeth inflicting wounds that are often fatal.

The Buffalo African buffalo live wherever there is water nearby, whether on the savanna or in the forest, in herds of up to 2,000. There are two types of buffalo in Africa: the big (1,870-pound), black Cape buffalo and the West African forest buffalo, a reddish brown animal less than half the size of its more aggressive relative. Buffalo are known for their bad tempers and are responsible for many human deaths and injuries each year. Most of these attacks are probably made by old male buffalo, which leave the herd and live in small bachelor groups. Buffalo herds are capable of defending themselves as a unit — if one herd member is caught by a leopard or lion, the whole group will rush in and attack the predator.

The Predatory Reptiles

The Crocodile and the Monitor Lizard The crocodile is the largest predator of the wetlands. Of the several kinds of crocodile, the one that is most dangerous to humans is the Nile crocodile. Up to 16 feet long, it is responsible for more human deaths than any other animal in Africa. It is designed for hunting, with sharp vision, acute hearing and a strong sense of smell. It eats mostly fish, but will also devour any animal it can wrestle into the water.

     The crocodile is a careful parent. For three months, females guard the clutch of eggs they've laid in the ground. When the young are ready to hatch, they bleat, and the mother digs up the eggs so that the hatchlings can crawl out of the nest. She then gently picks up the babies in her jaws, a few at a time, and brings them to the water. She will continue to guard them for about six weeks. Males will care for babies too, but the females usually don't give them the chance. Protective as they are toward young crocodiles, males also jealously guard their territory and may kill and eat other males that intrude.

Many other reptiles — turtles, snakes and lizards — live in or close to the water, as well. The Nile monitor lizard is another fairly large predator of the wetlands, eating creatures up to the size of small mammals.

Birds

The wetlands of Africa swarm with birds. Most lakes are home to groups of pelicans, marabou storks, herons, egrets, ibis, cormorants, darters, coots, grebes, Egyptian geese, many kinds of ducks, plovers, fish eagles and numerous other birds. In addition, there are birds that migrate to southern Africa to escape the cold European winters, and these visit the chain of lakes in East Africa's Great Rift Valley.

The Flamingo A flock of flamingos is one of the most impressive sights a bird lover could see in Africa. Huge flocks of these beautiful pink birds mass upon the salt lakes of the Great Rift Valley in flocks that number in the hundreds of thousands. Fish and mammals can't live in these lakes, but the waters form the perfect environment for the microscopic plant life that is the only food of the lesser flamingo. The greater flamingo also eats small shellfish and insect larvae, so it can survive in fresh water as well. Flamingos use their strange bills as sieves to strain the tiny plants and animals they eat from the mud and water.

The Pelican and the Stork Pelicans are another common sight on Africa's waterways. With long, straight bills connected to flexible pouches of skin, they are designed for catching and eating the many species of fish that fill Africa's waters. They are migratory birds — great white pelicans will fly for long distances between lakes, with as many as a thousand birds meeting in one place. They cooperate in hunting, swimming together in large rafts to herd schools of fish into the shallows so that they can scoop them into their pouches.

Many kinds of storks are often seen in the wetlands. Their diet is not very specialized — they eat anything, up to the size of small mammals, that they find in swamps and marshes. The white stork is the best known of the species, and the best protected. The marabou stork is a scavenger. It often hangs around human dwellings, looking for garbage.

Parks

Many other animals can be seen in the beautiful protected wetlands of Botswana, Kenya, Tanzania, Uganda and Zambia. One unique area is Botswana's Okavango Delta, the largest inland delta in the world. This lush sanctuary is found, surprisingly, in a country that is largely semidesert. In the northeast of the delta is the Moremi Wildlife Preserve, 1,160 square miles of swamps, islands, flood plains and forests, as well as dry land. This area abounds with antelope, aquatic predators, as well as predators usually found in the plains and forests, and big game. The Linyati Swamps of Chobe National Park are filled with papyrus, a plant

from which paper was made in ancient Egypt. Kenya has the lakes of the Great Rift Valley to attract huge bird populations. Tanzania has Lake Manyara, a salt lake.

Uganda has numerous lovely wetland areas, since one-sixth of the country is covered by water. Unfortunately, many animals were exterminated in the 1970s during Idi Amin's rule and the war that followed. But wildlife seems to be slowly coming back, and there are some species that are not found anywhere else, such as the pygmy antelope.

Zambia's Kafue Park is one of the largest parks in Africa, and it is the only home of the elegant antelope called the red lechwe. Since lechwe like to wade, lions in this park have learned to hunt in the water. Zambia has devoted 32 percent of its land to protecting wildlife, a trend that will be vital in saving Africa's fragile habitats and endangered wildlife.

The Desert

The Land

The shifting dunes of the desert appear bare of life. But most savanna dwellers can venture into these arid areas, and some animals make their homes here permanently.

The Sahara is the world's largest desert, stretching across Africa from the Atlantic Ocean through Egypt to the Red Sea. This is a sand-dune desert, with little vegetation and temperatures of up to 136 degrees Fahrenheit. Rainfall is sudden and severe when it oc-

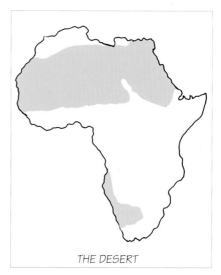

THE DESERT

curs. The thinly scattered plant life includes hardy trees and shrubs such as acacia, betoum, tamarisk, and jujube, as well as the delicate flowering plants that appear with the rain and disappear soon after. In the oases can be found oleander and tamarisk, and date palms that were introduced by humans.

The animal inhabitants of the Sahara include gazelles, oryx, addaxes and other antelopes, jackals, foxes and badgers. The lions that used to live in the Sahara were exterminated by the 20th century.

The Sahara's southern counterparts are the Kalahari and Namib deserts. The Kalahari is made up of reddish sands covered with some short, hardy grass. This desert is crossed by ancient river beds, and when it rains, these fill with water and stay filled for a few months. When this happens, the desert is visited by game animals. It is perhaps not accurate to call the Kalahari a desert, because it does include a great deal of plant life. The north and west are covered with dense scrub and scattered thorn trees, and an occasional tall palm can be seen. Watermelons and plants with large tubers that store water underground are common, a fact well known by the few Bushmen and Hottentots who live there. Because there are plants available, a surprisingly large number of animals can live in this arid place.

The Namib has little rain, but the sea breeze that sweeps up the western coast of southern Africa produces fog that provides moisture for the plants. One such is the welwitschia plant, which may live for up to 2,000 years. In general, this is not a hot place — it is called a desert for its lack of rainfall and surface water, rather than because of its temperature.

The Plant Eaters

The Horses: Grevy's Zebra, the Nubian Wild Ass and the Somali Wild Ass

A few types of wild horses make their homes in the desert. The zebras of the desert are larger and more densely striped than the ones found on the savanna. Grevy's zebra is found in the arid parts of the Horn of Africa that extend from Ethiopia to northern Kenya. It is a beautiful animal, taller than the common zebra, with narrower stripes set close together, and is becoming rare. Other horses are the Nubian wild ass and the Somali wild ass, dwellers of the deep desert. They look something like donkeys. Desert tribesmen try to mate wild stallions to their own mares to produce stronger, faster domestic horses.

The Antelope Oryx are antelope that are adapted for living in the deep desert. They are large, weighing over 400 pounds, with scimitar-shaped horns. They are social antelopes, living in groups. In Kenya, work is being done to domesticate these animals and use them like cattle in dry areas.

The Meat Eaters

The Dogs: The Jackal and the Fox The black-backed jackal is one of the predators found regularly in the desert. It is a scavenger, like its plains relatives. Other predators of the desert are of the fox family. The bat-eared fox is a tiny creature of the Kalahari and the Horn of Africa that uses its huge ears to locate the insects that it eats. Ruppell's fox is a small, large-eared fox found mainly in the Middle East but also in northernmost Somalia and in the desert fringes of the Sudan. The pale sandfox lives in Ethiopia and Somalia.

The Hyena The aardwolf, a highly specialized relative of the hyena, lives in the Kalahari Desert. It can also be found on the Cape of Africa. The aardwolf long ago removed itself from competition with other carnivores by becoming an insect eater, concentrating on termites. Unlike its striped and spotted relatives, it doesn't need strong, crushing molars, so its teeth have dwindled to small pegs. The striped hyena lives in arid environments other than the desert and is a scavenger.

Birds, Reptiles and Insects

The Ostrich The ostrich, the largest living bird, makes its home in dry habitats. It is striking, standing nearly eight feet tall and weighing as much as 300 pounds. It cannot fly, but, capable of running at speeds of up to 50 miles per hour and keeping that pace up for long distances, it can outdistance most predators. Lions approach it warily, because it can deliver lethal kicks with its long legs. Its eggs too are huge, equal in weight to two dozen chicken eggs. (Desert people use these eggs, hollowed, to store water in.) This bird uses its keen eyesight to spot the lizards and turtles it eats. Many of these small hunted animals avoid the midday heat by burrowing underground or staying under rocks.

Sharing the land with these animals are the smaller desert residents: horned viper snakes, fringe-toed and spiny-tailed lizards, gerbils and the similar jerboas, mourning wheater birds, and many kinds of insects.

Parks

The Kalahari Desert covers 80 percent of Botswana and is a protected wildlife area. Because of its vegetation and seasonal water, it is visited by such antelopes as springbok, gemsbok and eland, as well as by giraffes and by large predators who follow the herbivores. Many protected savanna areas include dry areas where animals suited to desert living can be seen.

Preserving The Gift

The animals of Africa are a gift to the world and need to be preserved both for their sake and ours. Every animal that disappears is a link gone in the chain that binds all living things together. It will be difficult to find the balance that will allow humans and animals to exist peacefully together on this continent that is struggling so hard to preserve the past while preparing for the future. In Africa's success, we will all be the richer.

PHOTO IDENTIFICATION ───────────────────────────────

(Cover) giraffes in Nairobi National Park\Kenya; (5) zebras; (6) leopard; (9) rhinos killed by poachers; (13) wildebeest and zebras on the Serengeti Plain\Tanzania; (14) white rhino\Angola; (15) lion; (17) vultures at Amboseli Park\Kenya; (18) ostriches; (21) elephants; (23) mountain gorilla\Rwanda; (24) juvenile mountain gorilla\Rwanda; (25) leopard; (26) parrot; (27) chameleon\Rwanda; (29) hippos; (39) buffalos and egrets; (31) crocodiles in the Zambezi River\Zambia; (33) flamingos at Lake Nakuru\Kenya; (34) a Thompson gazelle; (35) waterbucks\Mozambique; (36) wildebeest and zebras on the Serengeti Plain\Tanzania; (38) eland\Tanzania; (40) vulture; (41) hyena, vultures, and Marabu stork; (42) ostriches\Kenya; (43) ostrich; (45) antelope\Rwanda

For More Information

For more information about preserving African wildlife, contact the following organizations.

African Wildlife Foundation
1717 Massachusetts Avenue NW
Washington, DC 20036

Wildlife Preservation Trust
34th and Girard Avenue
Philadelphia, PA 19104

World Wildlife Fund
1250 24th Street NW
Washington, DC 20037

Appendix

The following animals are endangered, vulnerable or rare. These categories are defined by the International Union for the Conservation of Nature and Natural Resources. *Endangered* animals are in danger of extinction if the reasons for their endangerment do not change. *Vulnerable* animals are animals soon threatened with endangerment. *Rare* animals are animals of which a small number exist; they are not now endangered or vulnerable, but are at risk.

Vulnerable

Addax
African elephant
African wild dog
Black colobus
Black rhinoceros
Brown hyena
Cheetah
Chimpanzee and
   pygmy chimpanzee
Gorilla
Lechwe
Leopard
Pygmy hippopotamus
Scimitar-horned oryx
Various parrots
Zebras — mountain and
   Grevy's

Endangered

African wild ass
Arabian gazelle
Arabian oryx
Cameroon clawless otter
Nile crocodile
Sand gazelle
Simien fox
Swayne's hartebeest
Various parakeets
Various parrots
Various red colobus monkeys
White rhinoceros

Rare

Hunter's hartebeest
Olive colobus
Various parakeets
Zanzibar red colobus

Glossary

Arboreal Refers to animals that live primarily in trees or the upper regions of the forest habitat.

Carrion The remains of animals that have died or been killed.

Carnivore An animal that eats mainly meat.

Desert One of the four main habitats found in Africa. It is a dry region with very little rainfall. The habitat is made up primarily of the Sahara, Kalahari and Namib deserts.

Desertification The process of turning a region into desert by destroying the vegetation in the area.

Forest One of the four main habitats found in Africa. It is made up of the large tropical rain forests, smaller swamp forests that grow around rivers, and mountainous forests.

Habitat The place where an animal or group of animals lives.

Herbivore An animal that eats mainly plants.

Nocturnal Refers to animals that are active mostly after dark.

Omnivore An animal that eats both plants and meat.

Poaching Illegally hunting animals.

Predator An animal that hunts other animals for food.

Preserves Protected areas where it is illegal to hunt animals.

Primates The group of animals that includes humans, apes, monkeys and related animals such as lemurs.

Savanna One of the four main habitats found in Africa. It is a vast grassland region.

Scavengers Animals and insects that feed mainly on scraps left over from other animals' kills. They are important because they keep the habitats clean by eating rotting meat and vegetation.

Slash and Burn The process of destroying large areas of forest by cutting down or burning the vegetation to make a clearing.

Wetlands One of the four main habitats found in Africa. Wetlands are located anywhere that there is a large body of water, such as a river or swamp. They can also be situated within any of the other three main habitats.

Index